Bridge Pamphlets
No. 1

BYE FOR NOW

LORRAINE MARINER

BYE FOR NOW

The Rialto

ACKNOWLEDGEMENTS

Some of these poems have appeared in *Magma, Soundings,* and *The Rialto* poetry magazines. 'Lieserl Einstein' appeared in *A Decade of Difference: Magma Poetry's Tenth Anniversary Anthology* (2005). Lorraine Mariner wishes to thank the Arts Council of England East, for a Writer's Award.

BRIDGE PAMPHLETS

This is the first in a series of *The Rialto* pamphlets designed to cross the gap between magazine and book publication for poets.

First published in 2005 by
The Rialto
PO Box 309 Aylsham Norwich
England NR11 6LN

ISBN 0952744473
The publisher acknowledges financial assistance from
the Arts Council of England, East.

The Rialto is a Registered Charity No. 297553
Typeset in Perpetua 10 on 12.5pt
Design by Starfish, Norwich www.starfishlimited.com
Printed by Printing Services (Norwich) Limited

For my mother and in memory of my father

CONTENTS

My Wedding 10
Beast 11
Say I Forgot 12
Swimming Lesson 13
Stars 14
Injured 15
Lieserl Einstein 16
Chair 17
Nine To Five 18
Assertiveness Role Play 19
Stanley 20
The Weather 21
Tonight On The Streets Of New York 22
After The Matinee 23
Journey Planner 24
Heart 25
Feathers 26
Mac 27
Bye For Now 28
Nuns 29
In My Shop 30
My Father's Soldiers 31
Tree 32
With The Beatles 33
Tea Cosy 34
There Is Nothing Wrong With My sister 36
Touched 37
In My Worst Moments 38

PREFACE

A part of the excitement of running a poetry magazine is the risk of discovery: the realization, opening up yet another envelope of poems, that *this* is it, the authentic achieved voice. It's like the sudden sight of a rare bird in a familiar hedgerow. I'm delighted to be publishing this selection of Lorraine Mariner's poems.

Lorraine is not a prolific poet - the envelopes with her poems in arrive at long intervals - and it has taken awhile for her to feel ready to take this step of pamphlet publication. This is partly because she is very careful of her writing - even while we have been putting these together she's made small changes to poems. It is this care and willingness to experiment, re-work, try for the best possible combination of words, that gives her work assurance. The longer poems are meticulously sustained, the shorter ones deceptively light. There's work here that deserves to be in every anthology of new poetry. A quiet voice, but one with a lot to say.

Michael Mackmin

MY WEDDING

Since discovering that I am due to be married
at a church in Preston on the fifteenth of September

I have decided to never again type my name
into an Internet search engine. That she will soon

be someone else is some consolation, while the thought
of her reading one of my poems is not, knowing

the shock I felt on finding I was living in Lancashire
and had changed denomination for the sake of Trevor;

the thought that maybe we are living each other's lives
and she would make a better poet, I a better Methodist.

BEAST

When I was a child I worried
that when I got my chance to love a beast
I would not be up to the task and I'd fail.

As he came in for the kiss I'd turn away
or gag on the mane in my mouth
and the fair haired prince
and the dress that Beauty wore
on the last page of my Ladybird book
would be lost to me forever.

But now I see that the last thing my father
driving home late from work
would have on his mind is the gardens
flashing past and he would never stop
to pick a rose for one of his daughters
and if some misfortune such as

his Volvo reversing into a beast's carriage
did occur and I ended up at the castle
as compensation, the beast would probably
just set me to work cleaning and I'd never
look up from scrubbing a floor and catch him
in the doorway admiring my technique.

Still, as I've heard my dad say
he and his children may not always
be brilliant but we always turn up,
and in time when the beast comes to realise
that I haven't tried to escape
he'll give me leave one Sunday a month

to visit my family and access
to his vast library, and in bed at night
reading by the light of a candle
I'll shut another calf bound volume
and hear its quality thud
with something like happiness.

SAY I FORGOT

Say I forgot how to love you, the way
when I was eight I forgot how to swim?
Could you steel yourself as my mother did
when she enrolled me in lessons for the holiday,
sat up in the stalls with a four-year-old
every morning for a month and afternoons
took me swimming herself in a learner pool
let me grip her hands willing me to let go?
I don't know what makes a child doubt
the water is able to keep her afloat,
think that the other side is too remote
but if I choked now, could you wait it out
until I'm paddling again towards your smile
and wrapped tight in your towel like the first time?

SWIMMING LESSON

I think it was Stuart, at the Upminster Windmill
standing beneath the slats of the wooden stairs
to look up the skirt of Michelle's mother
as she descended sideways in high heeled sandals.

And I'm certain it was Stuart nudging me in class
to look down the cleavage of Miss Bowler
bent over us in her bold flowered summer dress
showing us how to do something I can't remember now.

And it must have been Stuart, holding on beside me
in Hornchurch swimming pool, which was how
I came to be looking up the shorts of our swimming instructor
while she stood on the side demonstrating

the correct way to move your legs during breaststroke.
That lesson was the kindest she'd ever been
possibly because of my wide eyed expression
which she took to be some kind of miraculous

conversion to the joy of swimming
when what she could actually see was terror
as I caught glimpses, as her leg circled
above my head, of the result of years of depilation

for a career spent in swimsuits, abandoned now.
The awful realisation that what I could see up there
was my future, the one that came after Miss Bowler's
beautiful breasts; and my leg technique must have been perfect

as I breaststroked past the instructor later that morning
trying to make amends for my betrayal, comprehending
another us and them apart from pupils and teachers,
and that I would never look again where Stuart was pointing.

STARS

The night I stayed at your parents' caravan where you
sprained your ankle giving your brother a piggy back,
we left you and your mother reading while your father
marched John and me along the beach, instructed

Look at the stars and I couldn't believe after
twelve years on this earth I'd never seen so many of them
up there and in spite of you laid out on your bed
we walked with our heads thrown backwards.

INJURED

At school I always wanted to get injured.
To have crutches and a whole group of new friends
trailing me at playtime, or stitches, or a serious illness
say diabetes (like my oldest friend Nicola's dad)

fussed over by the mother of a birthday party
with my own special plate of sugar-free finger food.
Like Katrina, who broke her arm one lunchtime
and was made to do PE that afternoon by her

unsympathetic teacher who always had her favourites
and didn't believe her. I know now
about the repercussions; the sprained ankle
biding its time until it twists again, the boy

everyone thought would play football professionally
until he went skiing, the scar. But the double whammy
of a visible injury and a negligent teacher –
when my forearm ached years later it would have been

a pleasure to remember the faces of Mrs. Hunt
and her pets, when I came in the next day
with my father wanting a word and my plaster cast
like an exclamation mark, white against the blackboard.

LIESERL EINSTEIN

That summer waiting to hear about my GCSEs
I worked in an ice-cream kiosk on the beachfront
and met a boy expecting to study maths in London
who had a way of putting Mr. Whippy in cones,
and away from the children dripping lollies along
the promenade, I let his fingers do sums on my skin.

Come September I was counting back the weeks,
trying to predict when the multiplication we had been
working on would be noticed, and I could understand
what my new physics teacher meant about the cat
in the box that's just been poisoned which you can't
be sure is dead until you lift the lid and take a look.

Throughout October there was morning sickness and
the cat was running around the house to the screams
of my mother, who called me a slut loud enough
for Mrs Evans and her hard hearing, while my father,
too stunned to remind his wife about the neighbours,
tore up my postcard of Saint Paul's Cathedral.

Now it's September again and I'm back at my desk,
my mother at home with her own second chance
another summer gone, a new law of motion learnt,
comparing hair and eyes, the way we sometimes cry,
and the boy from the kiosk comes home when he can
and demonstrates that he also has a way with bottles.

Tonight, when you finally slept, I read about Einstein
and how even he with his head for figures could make
the classic miscalculation and get his girlfriend pregnant;
but they gave their daughter away, a wrong answer.
We will work this out. You are simply someone new
among our number that we need to take account of.

CHAIR

The staff room where I used to sit has a chair in it,
different from all the other chairs, where my boss always sat.
The chair was there before she came; it wasn't her chair,
but she always sat in it and the rest of us never sat in it,
even when she wasn't there, because it had become her chair.

Of the other chairs, I often found myself drawn to one
that looked out of the window, but when I noticed my boss
sitting in the same different chair each break time, I tried
to make myself sit in a different same chair and appreciate
the walls, and my career goal became, 'Never be chair-tied'.

If you read this and find yourself sitting in a staff room in a chair
you always sit in or which you feel you should sit in, turn and say
This is not my chair to the person sitting alongside you. Or if you
read this and find yourself looking at a chair you would like to sit in,
please stand up and get out of there as quickly as you can.

NINE TO FIVE

In this envelope I have placed my future hopes
for my life as an OAP. After imagining
how my weeks will be spent when I get to sixty –
a slow walk to the paper shop each morning
and occasional cruises – I have opted for the Classic
over the Premium scheme. In another envelope

which the Pensions Officer will never see
is my application to the Dolly Parton School
of Old Age. This is the place where they help you
to write a classic song which eighteen years later
is covered by the star of a Hollywood film, who
puts it at number one in the charts for half a year.

With the royalties you build a Tennessee theme park
and continue having the plastic surgery that began
with double D breast implants. You spend your retirement
singing and being witty on chat shows to promote
your latest album until you wake up one morning
look in the mirror and think *What in the name*

of bluegrass! at the sight of your baby smooth face
when the look in your eyes tells you you're ninety.
On that day I will dress, with help, in my finest
wig, waistcoat and fringed boots, drive
in a golf buggy to the roller coaster designed
with my enormous boobs in mind and say

Buckle me in boys to the teenagers on duty.
Then, after the slow ascent, I will pause on the tip
of one of my breasts, scream *I will always love you*
and as my collagened lips spread flat and my curls
and sequinned Stetson hat lift off from my head
I will leave this life in the dip of my cleavage.

ASSERTIVENESS ROLE PLAY

I am your work colleague, neighbour and friend.
I have a dog. I'm always going away for the weekend
and expect you to look after my dog which means
you can't go anywhere. You've had enough.
I say *Hi Michael. How are you?* You say *Fine.*
I say *I'm off to Rome.* You say *That's nice.*
I say *I'll drop Rover round on Friday.* You say *No*
and use your broken record; *Lorraine, I'm sorry,*
I'm not going to look after your dog any more.
I want to be free at the weekend. I'm supposed to
keep asking and you're supposed to keep saying
I'm not going to look after your dog again
but instead you touch my leg and say *Ok*
bring round your dog. How can I refuse you?
The trainer is not impressed. She doesn't think
you're taking this course seriously. The other pairs
are still in role so we have time to kill and I ask you
if you like dogs and you tell me you don't because of
a stupid Afghan Hound you had as a child, while
the part of me deep inside that knows what it wants
says *Forget my dog. He's a figment of the trainer's*
imagination - you are not. I noticed when we had
to share one thing we like to do, with the group
at the start of the course, yours was going to an
Italian class. Well, I'm learning the language too
only I didn't like to say in case you thought I was
making it up but... vieni a Roma con me.
This will be my broken record; *Come with me to Rome.*
I've never been and the ice cream I'm planning to eat
on the Spanish Steps is too big for one. To show
that we mean business the trainer says we need a limit,
something that we will do if our needs don't seem
to be getting met. Not an empty threat. What you say
you have to see through. *Michael, come with me to Italy*
or my dog will bite you. Or I will. My bottom line.

STANLEY

Yesterday evening I finished
with my imaginary boyfriend.
He knew what I was going to say
before I said it which was top of my list
of reasons why we should end it.

My other reasons were as follows:
He always does exactly what I tell him
Nothing in our relationship has ever surprised me
He has no second name.

He took it very well
all things considered.
He told me I was to think of him
as a friend and if I ever need him
I know where he is.

THE WEATHER

How's this getting to know people better,
pointing out we're experiencing rain?
I must stop talking about the weather.

They know themselves the day is pleasant
they've got eyes in their head and a brain.
How's this getting to know people better?

It's not as if I sound very clever
I don't use technical terms to explain.
I must stop talking about the weather.

I haven't owned a garden ever
to be talking of shoots and frost in vain.
How's this getting to know people better?

If they're cold they put on a sweater,
if they're hot they take it off again.
I must stop talking about the weather.

I swore I'd stop this unnecessary blether
but a pause in our talk and I can't refrain.
How's this getting to know people better?
I must stop talking about the weather.

TONIGHT ON THE STREETS OF NEW YORK

Tonight on the streets of New York
it is so cold that if you cried
the tears would freeze on your face
and a stranger might pluck them off
and make you a necklace

and going into a Manhattan bar
when you took off your scarf
the bartender would watch the glass beads
melt around your throat
and pour you a Jack Daniels before asking.

AFTER THE MATINEE

After Edward Hopper's painting 'New York Movie', 1939.

I will go to the ladies restroom,
take the uniform trousers off
I'm wearing over my stockings, over these
strappy shoes, put on my black satin dress,
reapply my make-up, smooth down my hair

and walk straight backed
through the foyer, handing my torch to Doris
behind the confectionery counter,
to where he is waiting outside
smoking by the ticket booth.

This time I will not be disappointed
when his automobile is not any model
Humphrey Bogart drives,
when the restaurant is not the sort
of establishment where Bette Davis dines

and when I thank him
for a lovely evening and we kiss
and there is no music before his lips
move towards mine... No, I will not cry
in my dark room whose curtains I never open.

JOURNEY PLANNER

You are not a tube for me to take,
not a line with a certain destination.
There's no pocket map of your system;
this ticket isn't valid any more.

But still I stand on the platform:
wait with books and an iPod,
ignore announcers advising alternatives,
keep checking the indicator board.

And if you come I'll mind the gap,
find a space and hold on tight.
Become accustomed to your motion –
expect you each morning, every night.

HEART

Then there was the night leaving the pub
where she lost her heart by slipping it
into his pocket as he did up his overcoat.

On the bus going home he bruised it
when he sat on it, thinking *My seat seems*
to be ticking? When he found it,
feeling for his door key, it was still warm.

After sleeping with it on his bedside table
he placed it next to his computer at work
until his boss pointed out it was upsetting
the other members of staff; *Why not a plant?*

In the evening he went back to the pub
to show the landlady, who pointed her out
slumped in the corner, blue in the face
barely breathing, to which he said *Fancy*

giving your heart away so easily! The landlady
agreed, so the kitchen staff cooked it, and he ate it
washed down with a pint of Guinness.

FEATHERS

With the woman from your office that you left her for
away at a weekend conference, you found yourself
at a party staring at your ex-girlfriend and her
new boyfriend, and deciding that the new boyfriend's
jumper was the kind favoured by train spotters or
watchers of birds (the sort that fly without any help
from you) repaired to the bedroom set aside for coats,
got as close as you could to the dressing-table mirror,
and practised saying *For old times sake* with your eyes.

But you didn't know that on the evenings you were
working late, she had put off going home to an empty flat
by browsing in a bookshop near the station, and read
in the poetry section that hope is the thing with feathers
and in the natural world section that ninety per cent
of bird species are monogamous compared with
three per cent of mammals, and bought herself a pocket
guide by Bill Oddie and binoculars one lunchtime from a
sports shop, and waited for the day when you would leave.

So when you approached her at the buffet table
your 'come to bed' look didn't register and you found
yourself demanding *Who's the fucking jumper?*

Refilling their glasses in the kitchen her new boyfriend
picked up that stunned silence in which he could have
told you about the day on Hackney Marsh
when from his hide he saw her walking towards him,
a new variety that he couldn't name, who wanted to learn
everything he could teach her and had him describe swans
mating for life again and again and again, and how much
she loves his jumpers, particularly this one,
bought by her and worn by him to repel birds of prey.

MAC

Eating in Regent's Park once more at his suggestion,
the last time that I saw him, I went to find the toilet
and when I came back he was wearing one of those
complicated outdoor pursuit macs, carried in his bag

ready for the rain, and I was amazed it fitted in there
but did not say, just zipped up my shower proof jacket
and hoped it wouldn't put me to shame, which it didn't.
But three months later, standing in another park, listening

and trying to see Radiohead, close to a man who had
the same sort of coat as his, and a wedding ring and a wife
who let her husband stand behind her back with his hands
in the pockets of her mac, it did. And soaked to my skin

walking back to the car, I decided I was going to get myself
a mac and a man like that, who would stand and hold me
by its pockets, regardless of the crap in them which I should
have binned, and I wouldn't get wet like this again.

BYE FOR NOW

Your repeated use of this phrase
at the end of emails
convinced me that we had a future

until I noticed that BBC
news readers and weather reporters
say it to sign themselves off

secure in the knowledge
that some percentage of the population
will still be there later on

even for the World Weatherview
at one o'clock in the morning
even if they're dead in their armchairs

waiting to be discovered by the neighbours.

NUNS

After I watched an Italian film
about a broken hearted woman
who became a nun I had a sense
for just a few minutes, walking
over Hungerford Bridge from
the National Film Theatre,
of what it might be like not to care
if anybody ever loved me again
because I had chosen to love Jesus
and I think what I felt was peace

so on the night I had to dress for
a Murder Mystery Dinner
as a glamorous nun I wondered
if I might get that feeling again,
but I was a moll disguised as a Sister
and all I felt was upset after my friend,
whose husband was my gangster lover,
told me I looked good in a habit
and I knew I was doomed with my
novice's body, floozy's heart.

IN MY SHOP

the changing rooms
will have mirrors
to make a Narcissus
of anyone

and there will be a queue
half a mile long
up the high street

while in the cubicles
curtains flung open
they will flick their hair
and turn and turn and turn.

MY FATHER'S SOLDIERS

I never really noticed my father's toy soldiers
until I brought a boy home and saw his reaction
to the armies lined up in their glass fronted cabinets.
I'd meant to ask my father some interested questions
such as which was his first regiment, which ones
had he painted and which were the rarest in terms of value,
because I understood about money and male teenagers.
But I never got round to it and am only remembering

all these years later now my father's in intensive care.
When the consultant said it was touch-and-go, I tried to imagine
death; and it was my uncle (who collects the opposition)
packing the soldiers back into their boxes, an advert
for an auction in 'Military Modelling' and my mother crying
over her husband's children, who don't know which little men
to keep for mementoes. I am inspecting the troops
while there is still touch and this miniature Empire stays.

Could it be these ones in blue tailcoats lighting canons
that are his favourites? Or these on horseback
with plumed hats and drawn swords? Or these, Greek
like my father's father, in white pleated skirts?
Their stoic faces try to persuade me that he loves them all
equally but at night, next door in my childhood bedroom
some of them call out to me *Where is our captain?*
I hear their tiny feet marching, marking time.

TREE

A year today, and I'm standing inspecting a sapling
in Kensington Gardens. Father, this is to be your tree
and though we wouldn't have found it without the map
from the Royal Parks Adopt A Tree, I've a sense of familiarity.

It's close to Soldiers Walk and you can just see the Round Pond
where you and your brother sailed toy boats together and my mother
says not far from here you made her play cricket, she bowled
to an oak, you batted with your black city gent umbrella.

Later we will walk to the sunken garden, then to the street
where you grew up, not the house, that would be too much
but Aphrodite's Taverna to toast Greece your team's victory
because dad, we supported them so well they've won the cup.

After you died I worried about my love for you, where would it go?
Eating stuffed vine leaves I think I know it's in the trees,
in the wood that could make a coffin, a ship, a pair of goal posts,
in the trunk of an ash we hope will grow, high as a cathedral

high as a long ball soaring above the Portuguese turf
kicked by a hero before a sea of fans in his blue and white shirt.

WITH THE BEATLES

Listening to The Beatles, does my mother
go back to the moment she first heard
'She Loves You' in her friend Pat's bedroom
and then queued after school at Woolworths?

And hearing *Rubber Soul* does she recall
afternoons with my dad and her portable player
him – looking a little like John Lennon –
itching to play his Dylan record?

Around *Sergeant Pepper* she says
it gets hazy, she was planning a wedding
buying a house, and when Paul McCartney
announced it was over she didn't really notice

she hadn't even bought their latest album;
but when she plays *Please Please Me* on vinyl
can she forget New York in December
or remember how love felt before my father?

TEA COSY

In my mother's kitchen is a tea cosy
made by her mother which has never
been used, and if I inherit it
as my mother did, I will not use it.

It won first prize in a craft competition
at Deal's over-sixties club and because
I was at school at the time and trying
to come first I thought it was fantastic

though we were not surprised because
my grandma was gifted that way
and all of us (me and my mum and dad
and my brother and baby sister) were

probably wearing the Aran sweaters
she had knitted for us when she held
up the tea cosy for us to admire
with hands knotted by arthritis.

It was made using green felt, lined with
something silky, also green, appliquéd
with a girl riding a bicycle, using wool
and pipe cleaners and actual twigs

which I imagine my granddad gathering
for my grandma because he was always
collecting plants, picking the odd flower
from someone's garden and planting it

in his own, but when my grandma died
he wasn't interested in their garden any more
and my mum told me that really
it was my grandma who loved the garden.

And if I don't inherit the tea cosy
(I now have two baby sisters) at least
I will have a poem about it
but knowing my sisters, as we sort

through my parents' possessions, over
tea in my mother's kitchen they
will remember I wrote a poem about
the unused tea cosy and let me have it.

THERE IS NOTHING WRONG WITH MY SISTER

After you told my sister that there was no one else
but you no longer wanted her, she went to bed
and tried to work out what she had done and
what was wrong with her and spent the night awake.

There is nothing wrong with my sister but may
there be something wrong with the Ikea wardrobe
she helped you to build so that tonight it falls apart
and wakes you from your unaccompanied sleep.

TOUCHED

Talking in the bar
on that last evening
I accidentally touched his knee
illustrating a point

and he moved it away
out of reach
towards the girl
sitting on his other side.

On our first evening
if I momentarily stroke your thigh
mid-conversation
do not be alarmed.

IN MY WORST MOMENTS

when I wondered whether to submit you to a magazine
I imagined myself a grand old lady of poetry
giving what many believed would be my last reading
at a distinguished hall somewhere in London.

I'd start off standing with a chair ready behind me
and there would be a lectern holding all my works
and I'd begin by reading from the period in my writing
that will bear your name in the definitive

biography of my life, from a first edition
of my first collection, which has been promised
along with the rest of my library and personal papers
to a university which I once attended. Suddenly

out of the corner of my eye through a cataract
I'd notice another old woman rising from the front row
and she would totter up the stairs to the stage and advance
on me, pushing a walking stick into my chest

demand *Leave my brother* or possibly *husband alone*
you lunatic and send me toppling into the arms
of the great new hope of British poetry who had
been asked to introduce me following an interview

in *The Independent* where he named me an influence.
Or maybe afterwards, signing copies of my books
in the foyer, you would shuffle up and rasp
What is the meaning of this you lunatic as you threw

the weighty volume that was my *Collected Poems*
on to the table. After you'd reminded me exactly
who you were, I could explain, if I'm able to remember,
that back at the turn of the century I'd suffered

from both you and poetry like a disease, but I won't.
So in the face of my silence you will grab me
by the throat of my high necked blouse with your
liver spotted hands and the poetry hope, who has been

standing beside me repeating people's names directly
into my ear, will have to intervene. Either way
I will end up in hospital being given a check-up
in view of my frailty but my niece or nephew

or maybe my son or daughter will notice my face
more animated than it has been for decades
as he or she straps me into their car to take me back
to the Hampstead flat I refuse to give up

and I will laugh and say *He touched me again*
after all those years and finally they will understand
that before they came along their aunt or their mother
really was the girl who wrote these poems.

Lorraine Mariner was born and grew up in Upminster, Essex, where she still lives. She studied English at Huddersfield University and Library & Information Studies at University College, London. She works at the Tate Library and Archive at Tate Britain. She started learning to write poetry in Huddersfield but the poems in this selection were written over the last six years.